AWESOME GOD

T0040831

— PIANO LEVEL —
ELEMENTARY
(HLSPL LEVEL 2-3)

ISBN 978-0-634-09322-7

HAL•LEONARD®
CORPORATION

7777 W. BLUEMOUND RD. P.O. BOX 13819 MILWAUKEE, WI 53213

Visit Hal Leonard Online at
www.halleonard.com
Visit Phillip at
www.phillipkeveren.com

PREFACE

Praise and Worship music is a vital part of the contemporary church. These songs are meaningful to worshippers young and old, and they will continue ministering to believers for generations to come.

We selected songs that have become classics in the church due to their inspired texts and music. These arrangements are tailored for the beginning level player, whether young or young at heart. We sincerely hope you'll enjoy playing them at home, in a worship service, or in recital.

Our God is an awesome God!

Sincerely,
Phillip Keveren

BIOGRAPHY

Phillip Keveren, a multi-talented keyboard artist and composer, has composed original works in a variety of genres from piano solo to symphonic orchestra. Mr. Keveren gives frequent concerts and workshops for teachers and their students in the United States, Canada, Europe, and Asia. Mr. Keveren holds a B.M. in composition from California State University Northridge and a M.M. in composition from the University of Southern California.

CONTENTS

4   ABOVE ALL

8   AS THE DEER

10   AWESOME GOD

12   EL SHADDAI

14   GIVE THANKS

16   GREAT IS THE LORD

20   HE IS EXALTED

26   HOLY GROUND

23   HOW BEAUTIFUL

28   I LOVE YOU LORD

30   LAMB OF GOD

34   LORD, I LIFT YOUR NAME ON HIGH

37   MORE PRECIOUS THAN SILVER

40   OH HOW HE LOVES YOU AND ME

42   SHOUT TO THE LORD

50   SHOUT TO THE NORTH

46   THERE IS A REDEEMER

53   WE FALL DOWN

ABOVE ALL

Words and Music by PAUL BALOCHE
and LENNY LeBLANC
Arranged by Phillip Keveren

Reverently

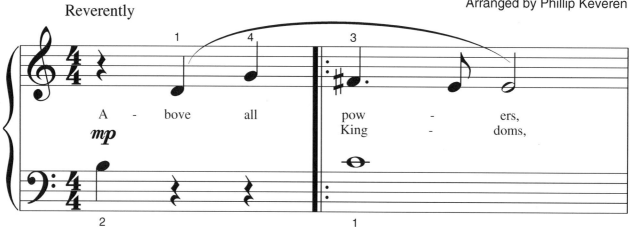

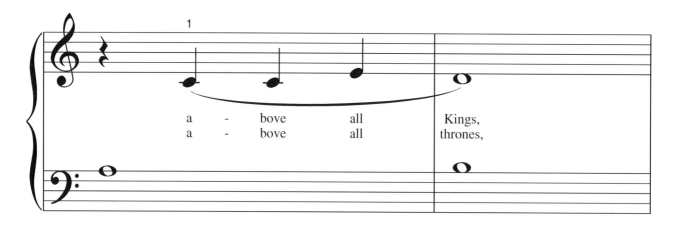

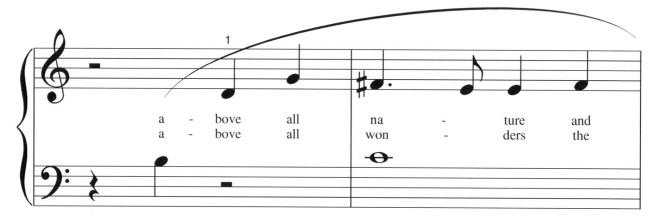

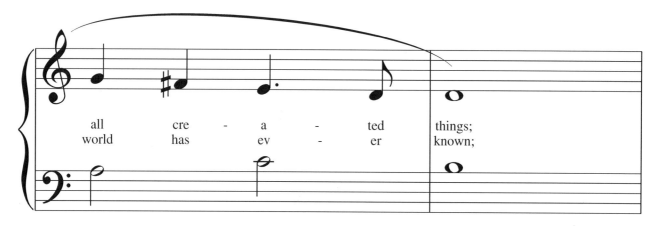

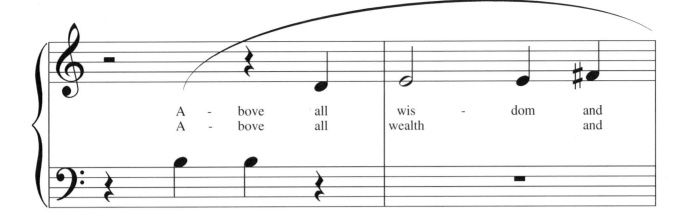

A - bove all wis - dom and
A - bove all wealth and

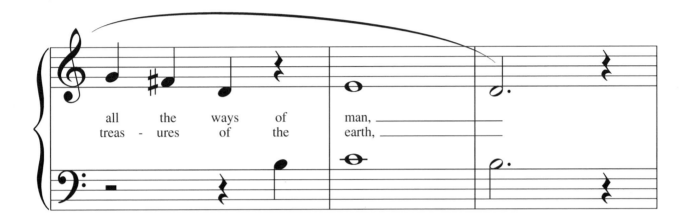

all the ways of man, _____
treas - ures of the earth, _____

You were here be - fore the world be -
there's no way to meas - ure what You're

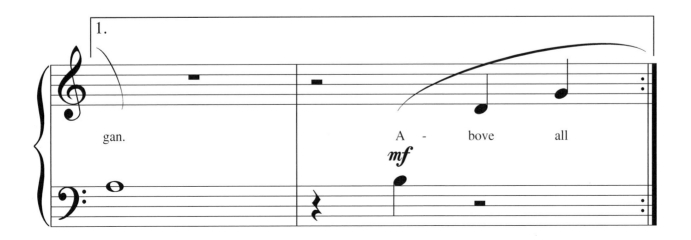

gan.

mf

A - bove all

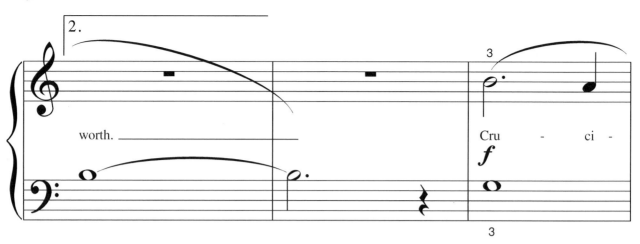

worth. _____ Cru - ci -

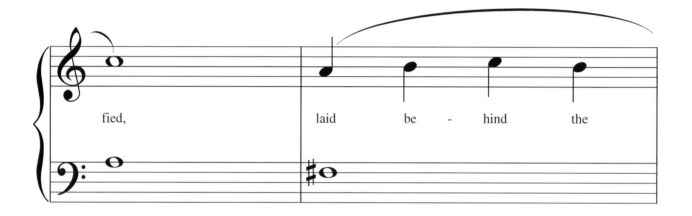

fied, laid be - hind the

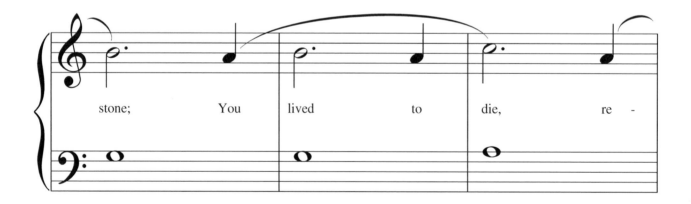

stone; You lived to die, re -

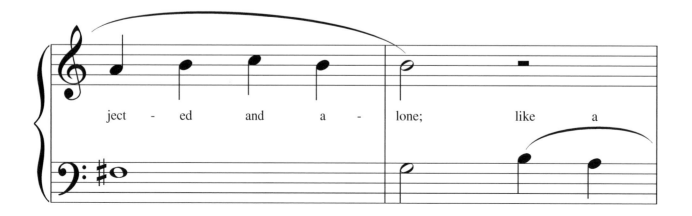

ject - ed and a - lone; like a

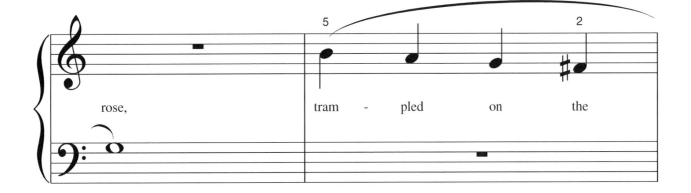

rose,   tram - pled   on   the

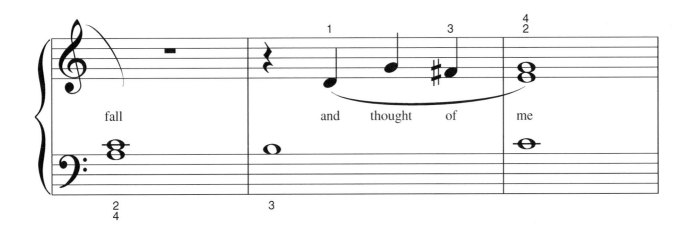

ground, _____   You   took   the

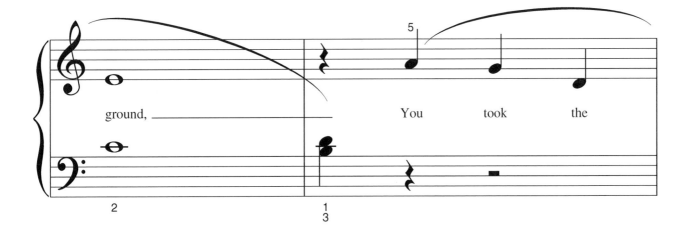

fall   and   thought   of   me

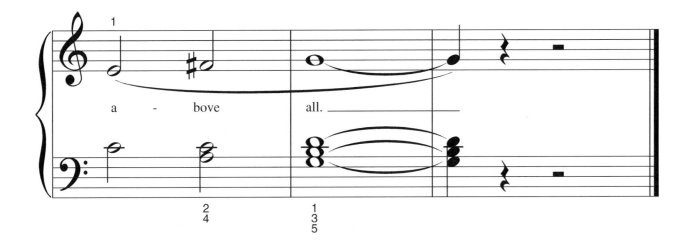

a - bove   all. _____

AS THE DEER

Words and Music by MARTIN NYSTROM
Arranged by Phillip Keveren

Tenderly

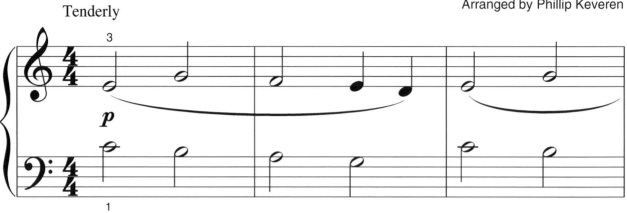

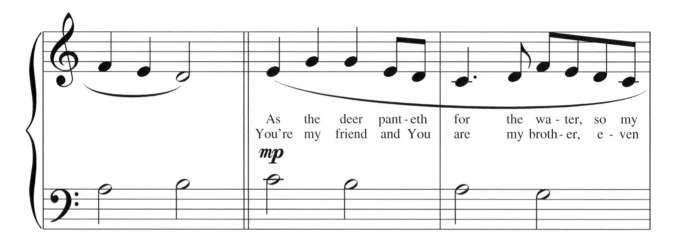

As the deer pant-eth for the wa-ter, so my
You're my friend and You are my broth-er, e-ven

soul long-eth af-ter Thee.
though You are a King.

You a-lone are my
I love You more than

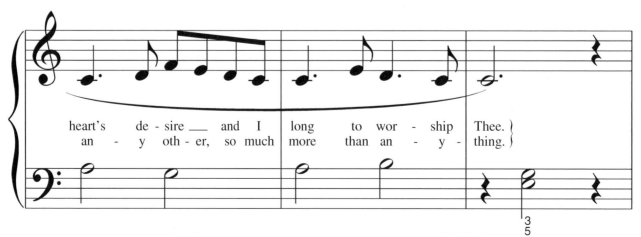

heart's de-sire __ and I long to wor-ship Thee.)
an-y oth-er, so much more than an-y-thing.)

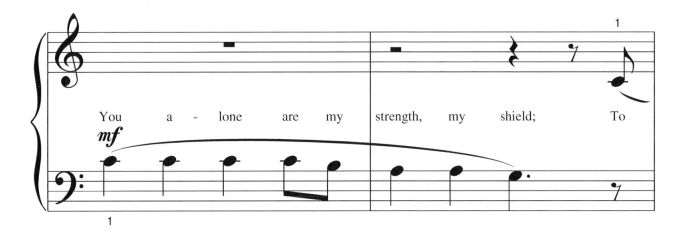

You a - lone are my strength, my shield; To

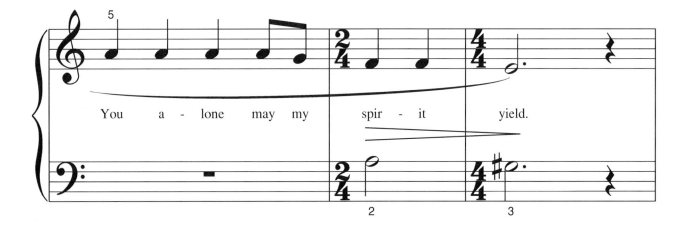

You a - lone may my spir - it yield.

You a - lone are my heart's de - sire ____ and I

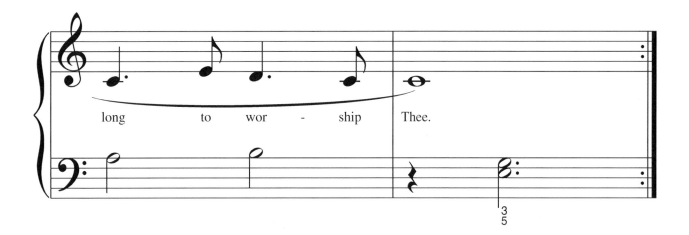

long to wor - ship Thee.

AWESOME GOD

Words and Music by RICH MULLINS
Arranged by Phillip Keveren

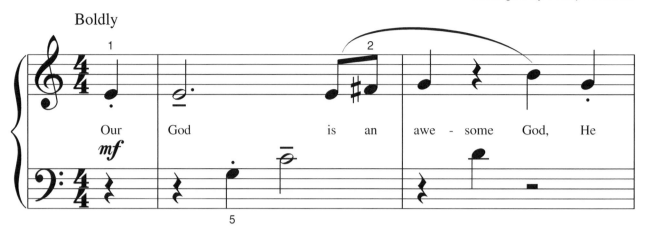

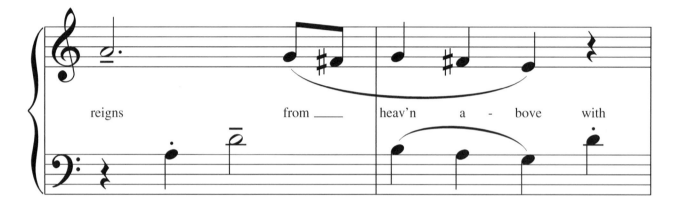

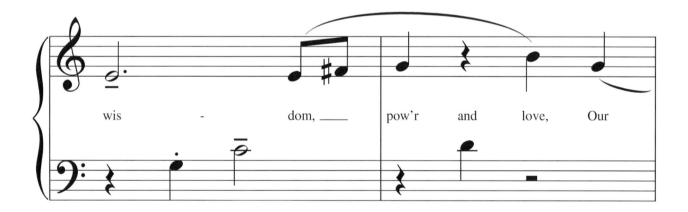

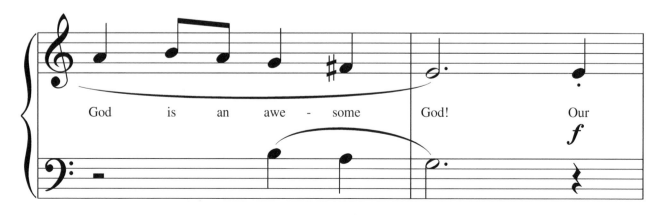

God   is   an   awe-some   God,   He   reigns   from __

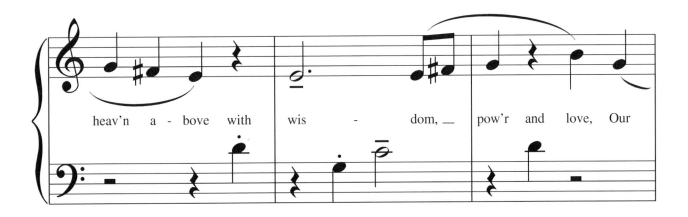

heav'n   a - bove   with   wis   -   dom, __   pow'r   and   love,   Our

God   is   an   awe - some   God!   Our

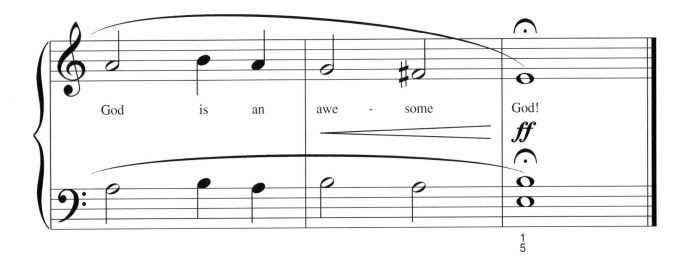

God   is   an   awe   -   some   God!

ff

EL SHADDAI

Words and Music by MICHAEL CARD
and JOHN THOMPSON
Arranged by Phillip Keveren

Singing

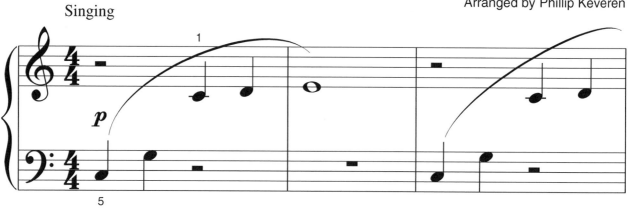

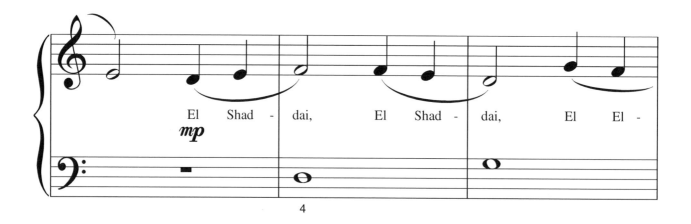

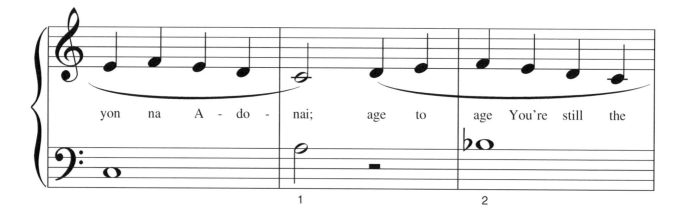

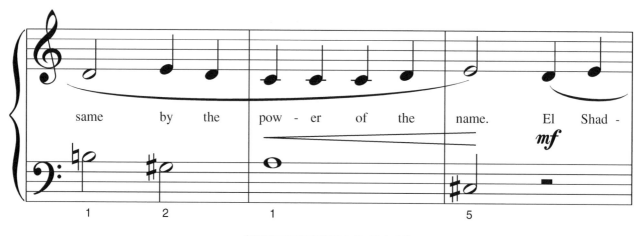

dai, El Shad - dai, Er - kahm - ka na A - do -

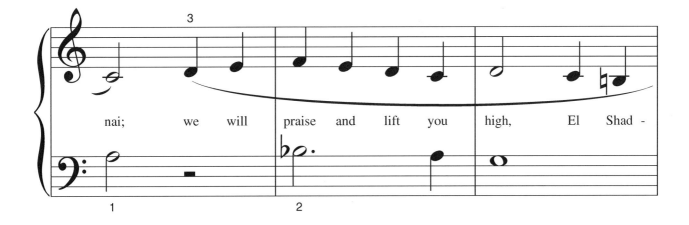

nai; we will praise and lift you high, El Shad -

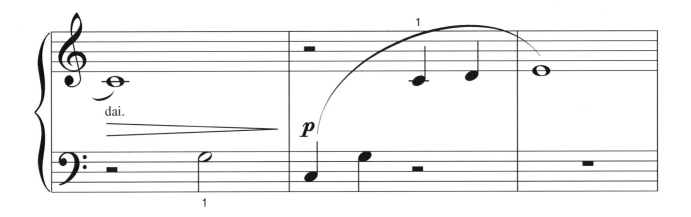

dai. *p*

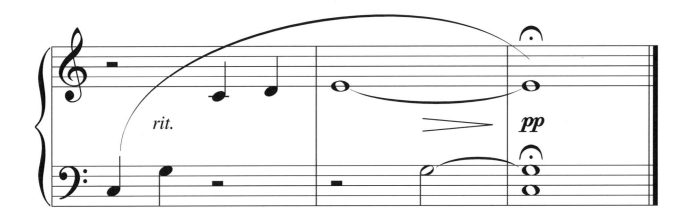

rit. *pp*

GIVE THANKS

Words and Music by HENRY SMITH
Arranged by Phillip Keveren

Gently

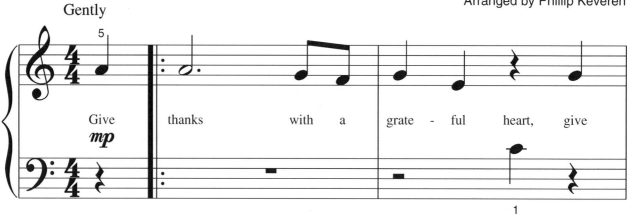

Give thanks with a grate-ful heart, give

thanks to the Ho - ly One, Give thanks _____ be - cause He's

giv - en Je - sus Christ, His _____ Son. And

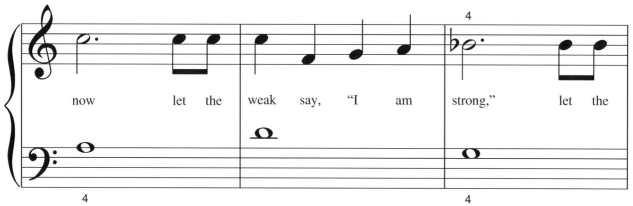

now let the weak say, "I am strong," let the

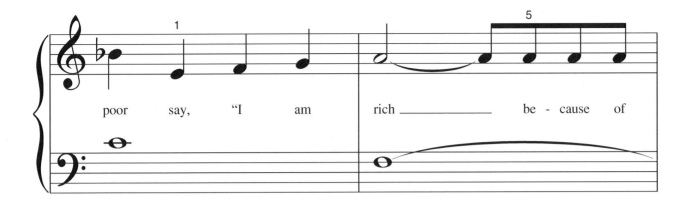

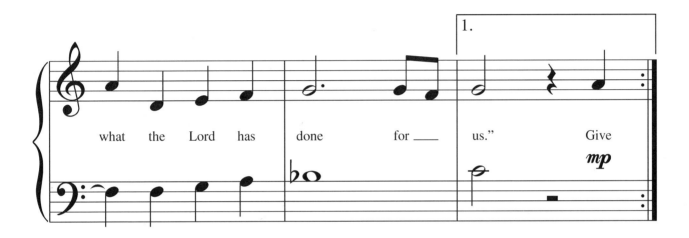

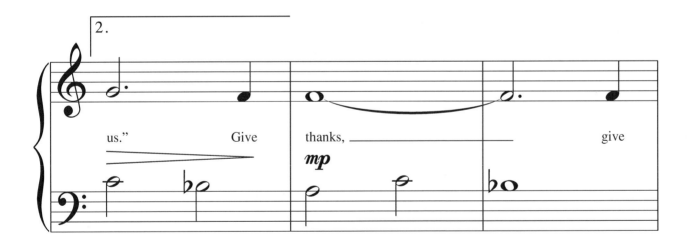

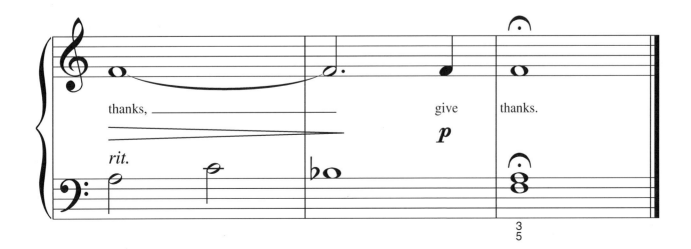

poor say, "I am rich _____ be-cause of

what the Lord has done for ___ us." Give

us." Give thanks, _____ give

thanks, _____ give thanks.

rit.

3
5

GREAT IS THE LORD

Words and Music by MICHAEL W. SMITH
and DEBORAH D. SMITH
Arranged by Phillip Keveren

Joyfully

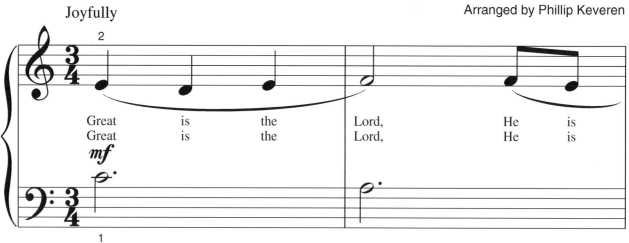

Great   is   the   Lord,   He   is
Great   is   the   Lord,   He   is

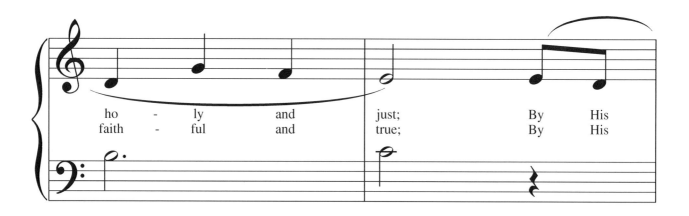

ho - ly   and   just;   By   His
faith - ful   and   true;   By   His

pow - er   we   trust   in   His
mer - cy   He   proves   He   is

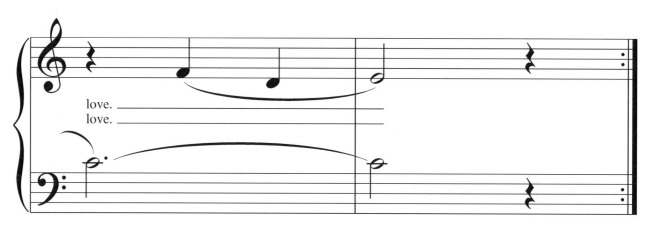

love.
love.

Great   is   the   Lord   and
wor - thy   of   glo - ry!

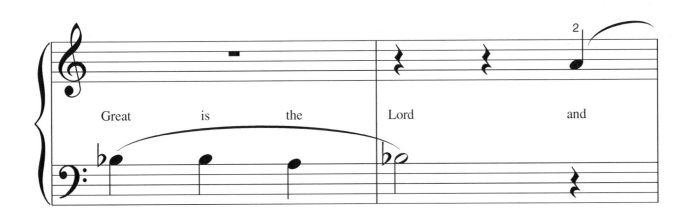

Great   is   the   Lord   and

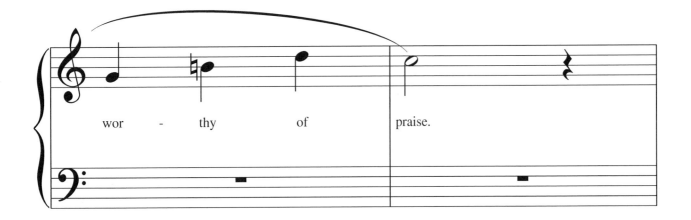

wor - thy   of   praise.

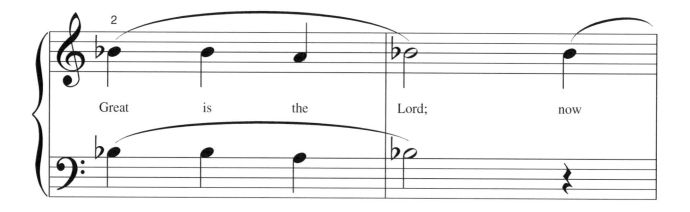

Great is the Lord; now

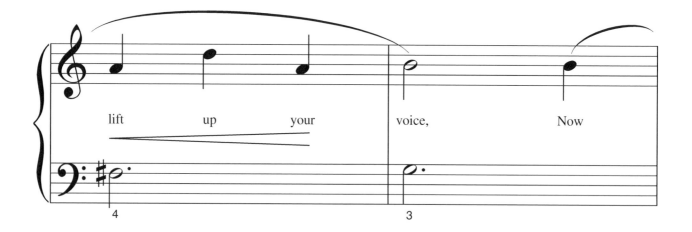

lift up your voice, Now

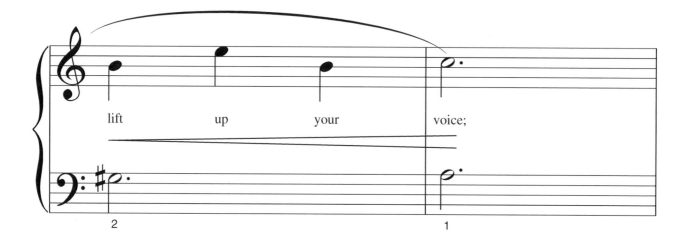

lift up your voice;

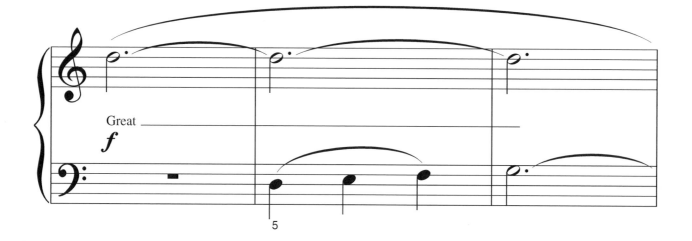

Great

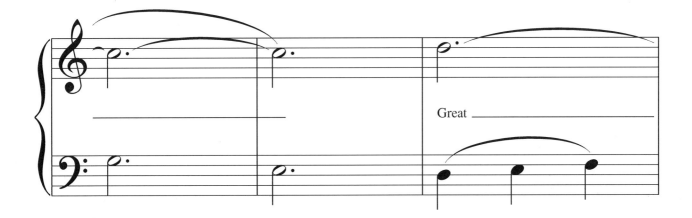

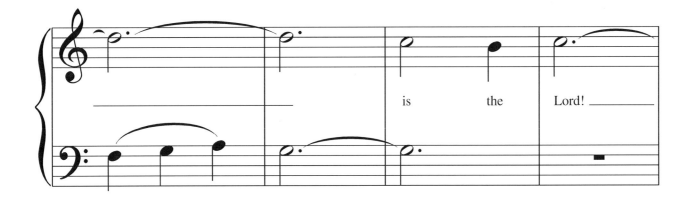

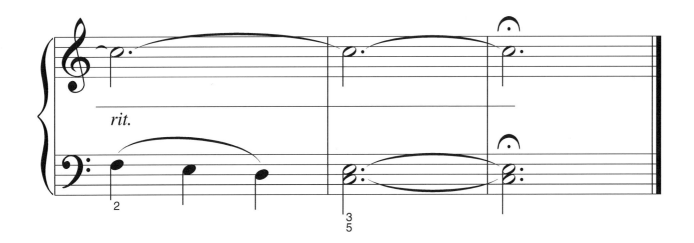

HE IS EXALTED

Words and Music by TWILA PARIS
Arranged by Phillip Keveren

Flowing

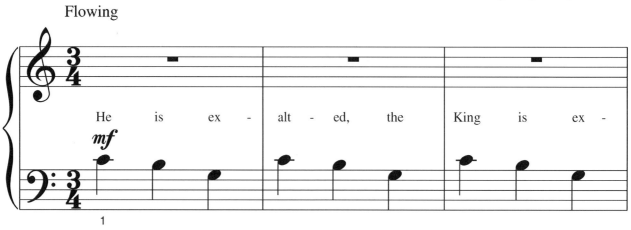

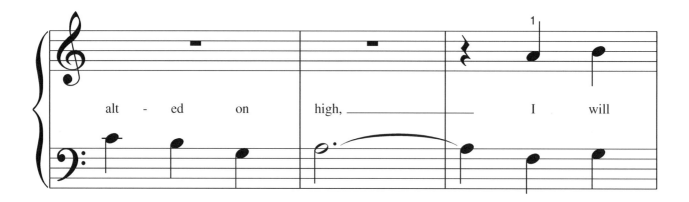

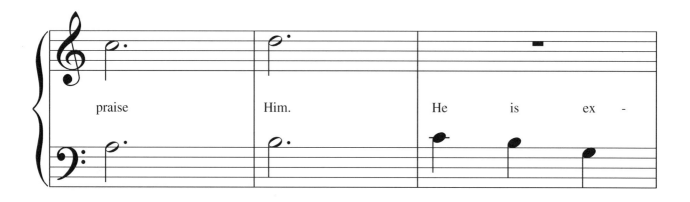

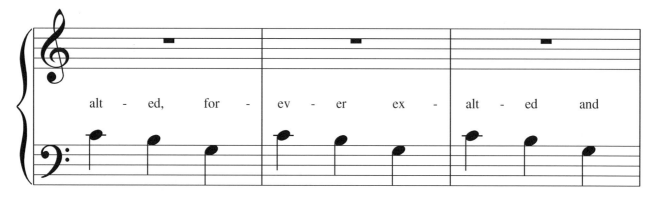

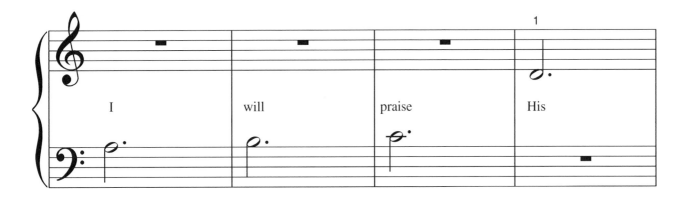

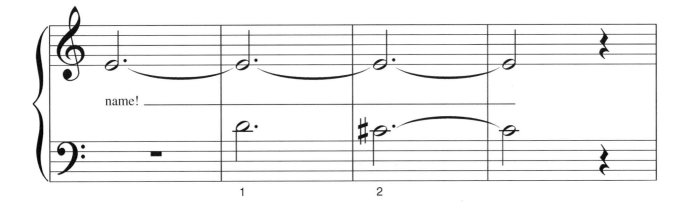

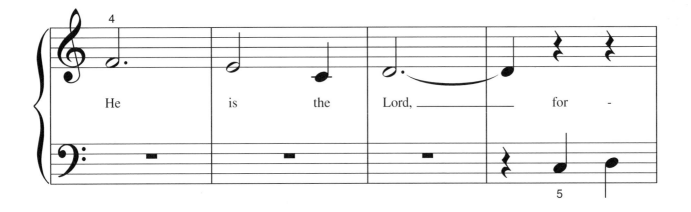

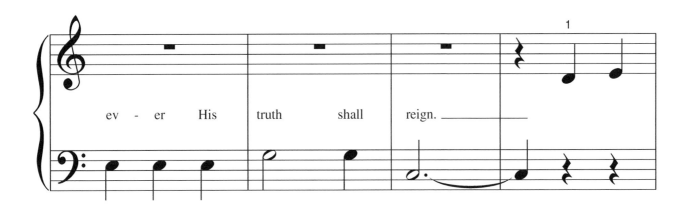

22

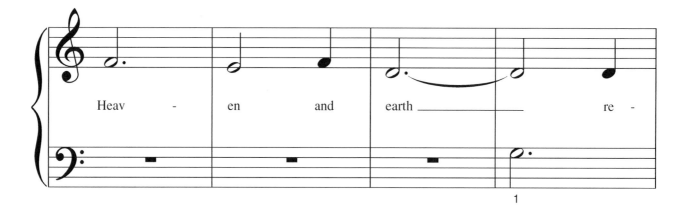

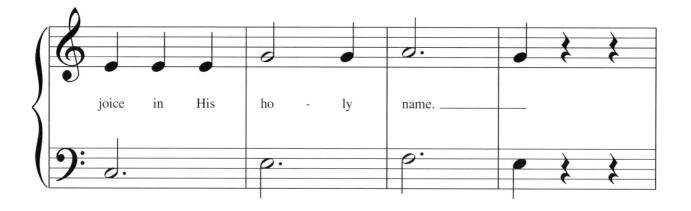

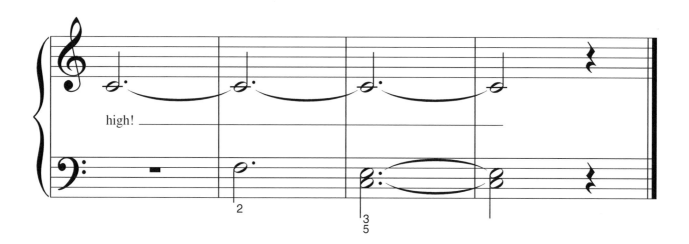

HOW BEAUTIFUL

Words and Music by TWILA PARIS
Arranged by Phillip Keveren

Gracefully

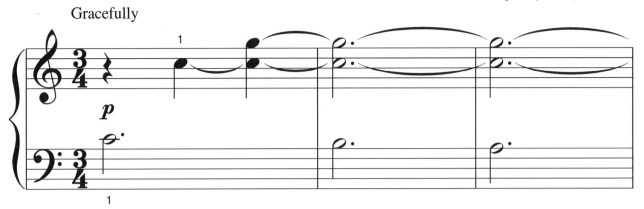

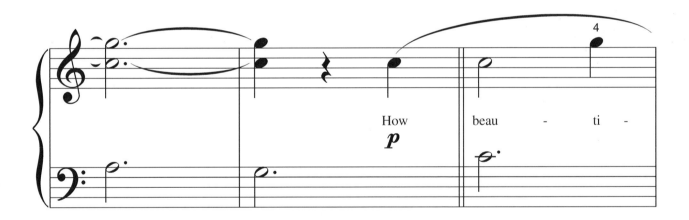

How beau - ti -

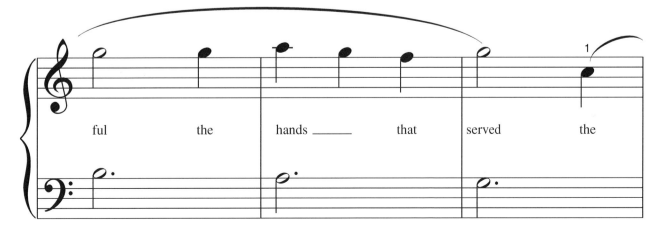

ful the hands that served the

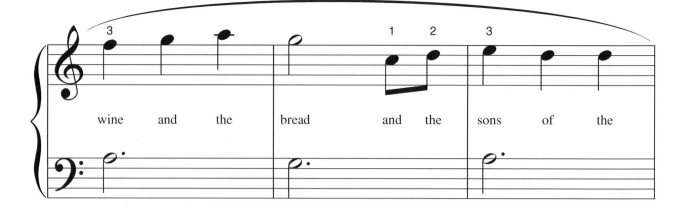

wine and the bread and the sons of the

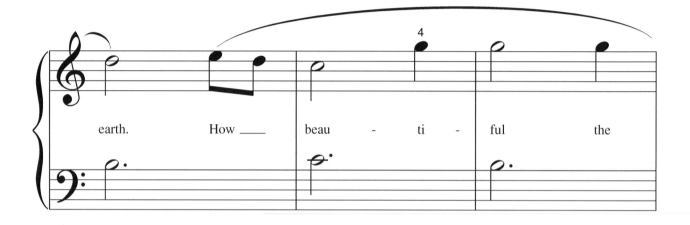

earth. How beau - ti - ful the

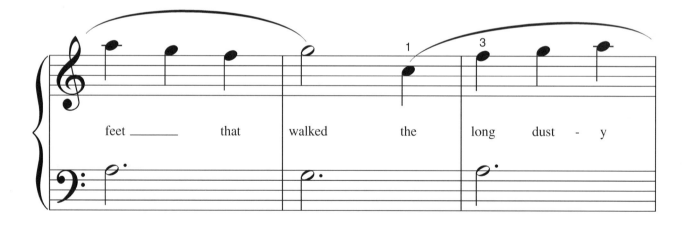

feet that walked the long dust - y

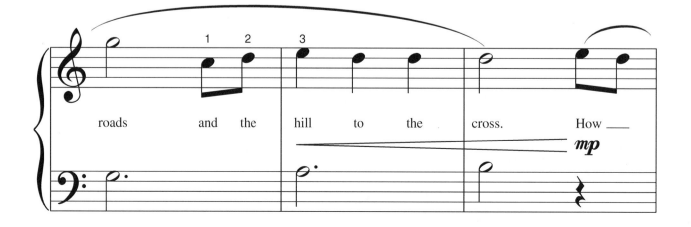

roads and the hill to the cross. How

mp

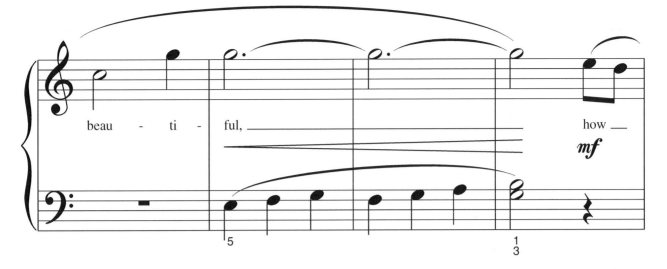

beau - ti - ful, _____ how _____ *mf*

beau - ti - ful, _____ how _____ *p*

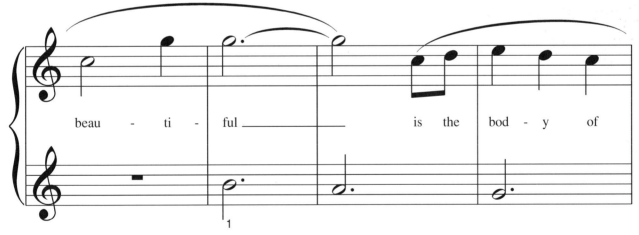

beau - ti - ful _____ is the bod - y of

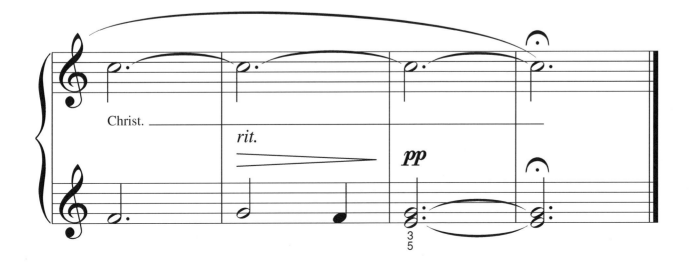

Christ. _____ *rit.* *pp*

HOLY GROUND

Words and Music by GERON DAVIS
Arranged by Phillip Keveren

Reverently

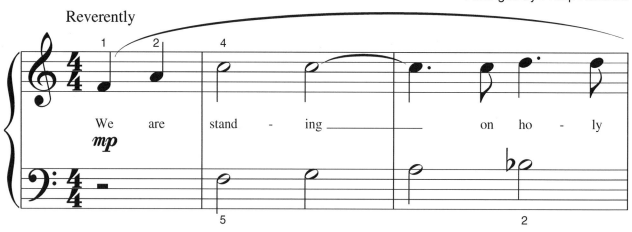

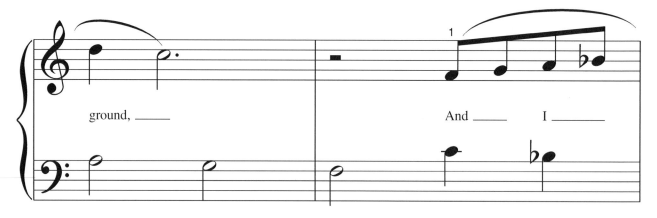

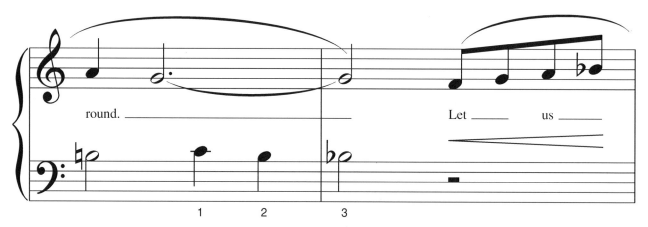

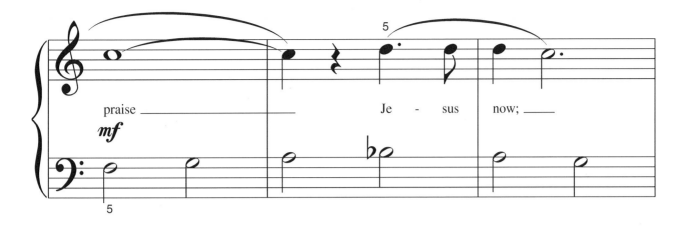

praise _____ Je - sus now; _____

mf

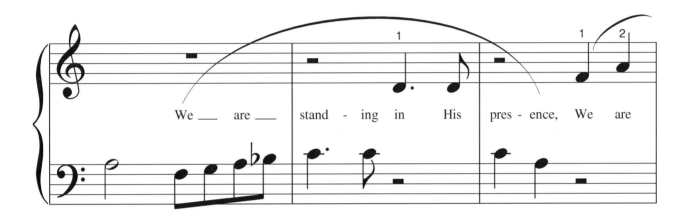

We ___ are ___ stand - ing in His pres - ence, We are

stand - ing in His pres - ence, We ___ are ___ stand - ing in His

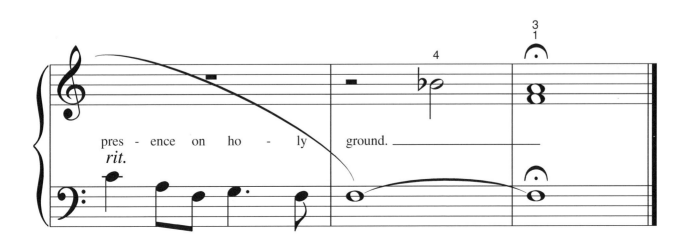

pres - ence on ho - ly ground. _____

rit.

I LOVE YOU LORD

Words and Music by LAURIE KLEIN
Arranged by Phillip Keveren

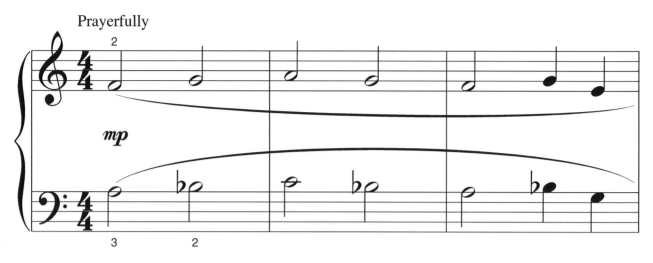

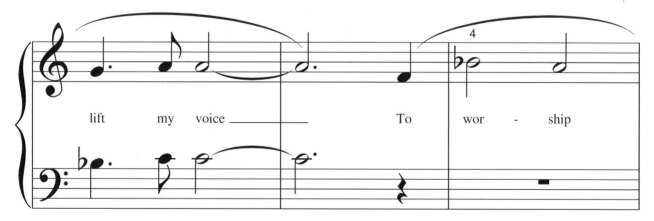

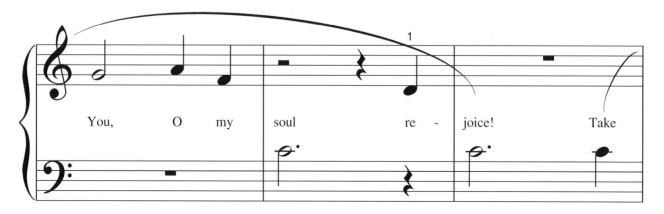

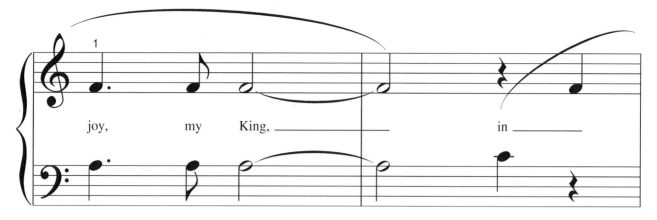

joy,   my   King, _____   in _____

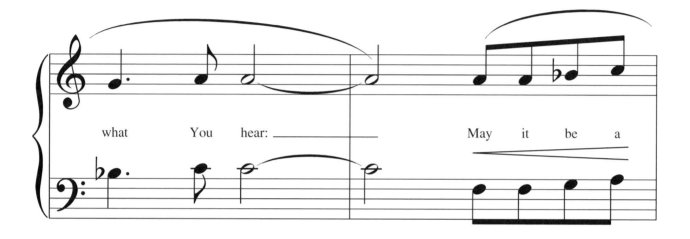

what   You   hear: _____   May   it   be   a

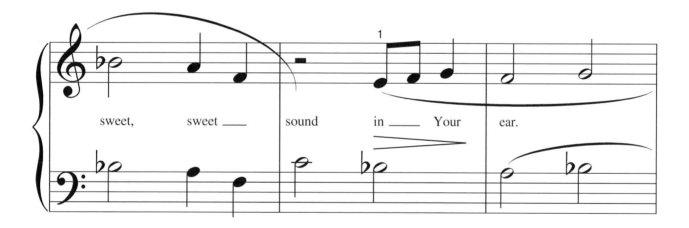

sweet,   sweet ____   sound   in ____   Your   ear.

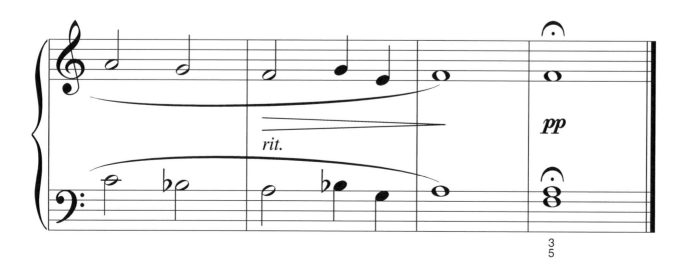

rit.   *pp*

LAMB OF GOD

Words and Music by TWILA PARIS
Arranged by Phillip Keveren

Gently

Your on-ly Son, no sin to hide, But You have

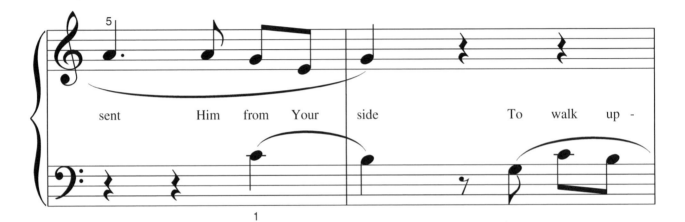

sent Him from Your side To walk up-

on this guilt-y sod, And to be-

come the Lamb of God. O Lamb of

God, sweet Lamb of God; I love the

ho - ly Lamb of God. O wash me

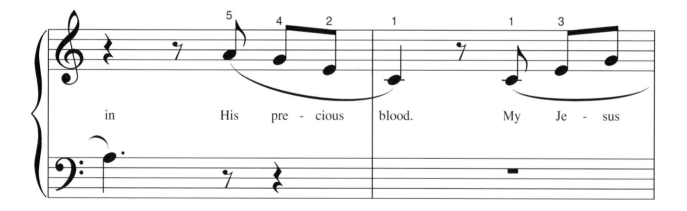

in His pre - cious blood. My Je - sus

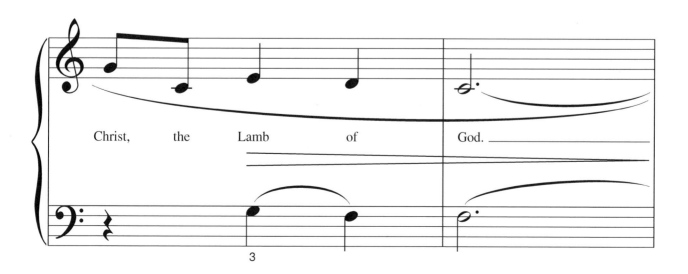

Christ, the Lamb of God. _____

32

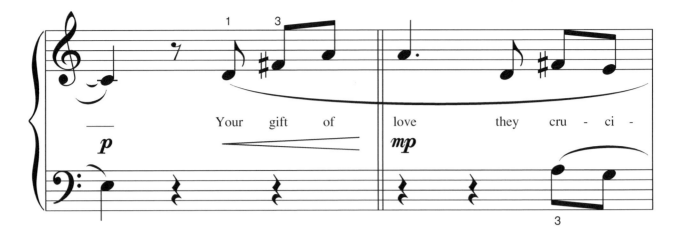

Your gift of love they cru - ci -

fied, They laughed and scorned Him as He

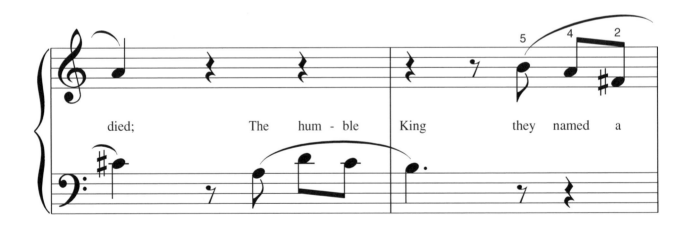

died; The hum - ble King they named a

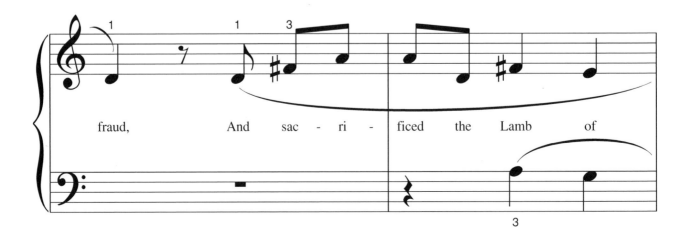

fraud, And sac - ri - ficed the Lamb of

God. O Lamb of God, sweet Lamb of

God; I love the ho - ly Lamb of

God. O wash me in His pre-cious blood. My Je - sus

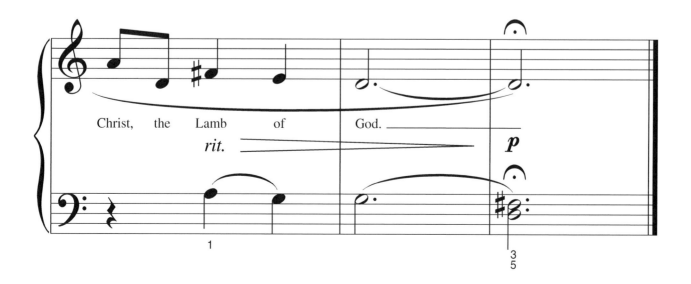

Christ, the Lamb of God.

rit. *p*

LORD, I LIFT YOUR NAME ON HIGH

Words and Music by RICK FOUNDS
Arranged by Phillip Keveren

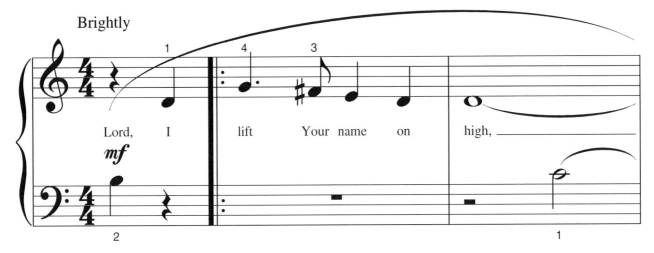

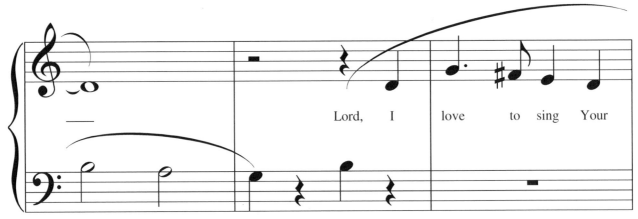

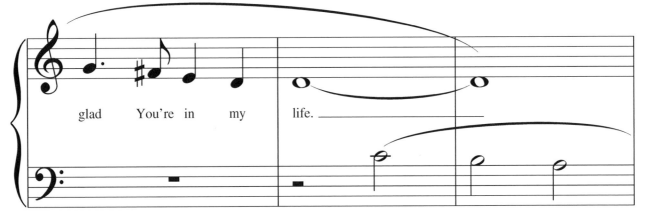

I'm so glad You came to save us. ____

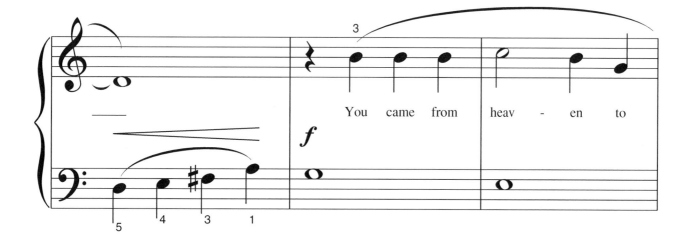

____ You came from heav - en to

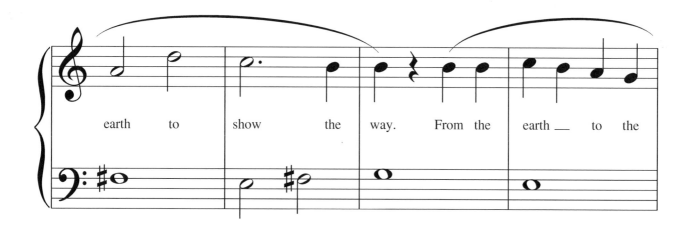

earth to show the way. From the earth ___ to the

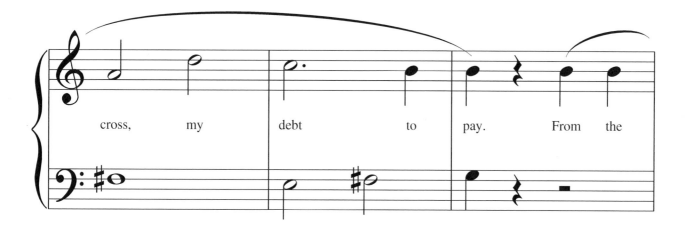

cross, my debt to pay. From the

36

cross ___ to the grave, from the grave ___ to the

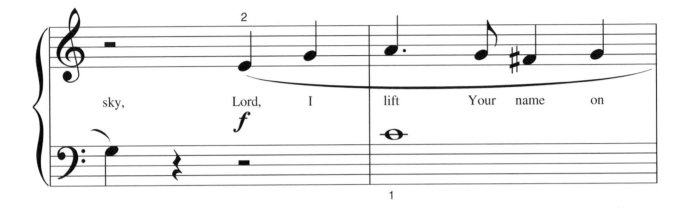

sky, Lord, I lift Your name on

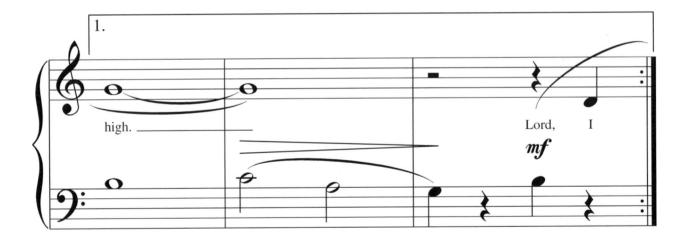

high. ___ Lord, I

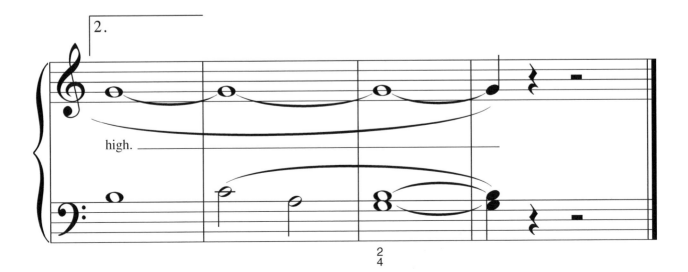

high. ___

MORE PRECIOUS THAN SILVER

Words and Music by LYNN DeSHAZO
Arranged by Phillip Keveren

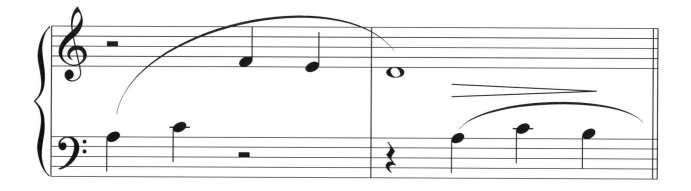

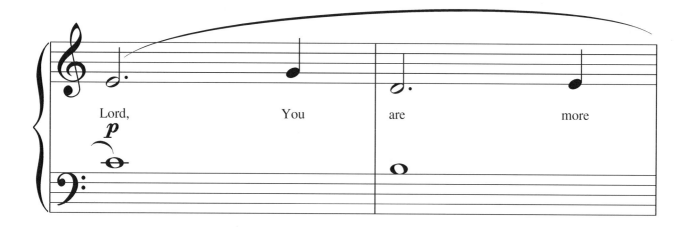

Lord,   You   are   more

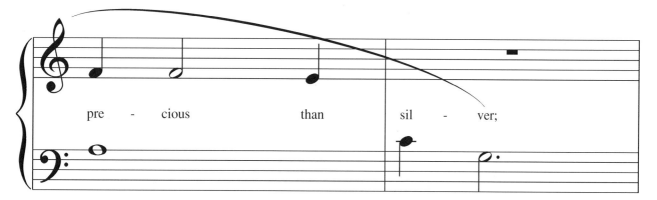

pre - cious   than   sil - ver;

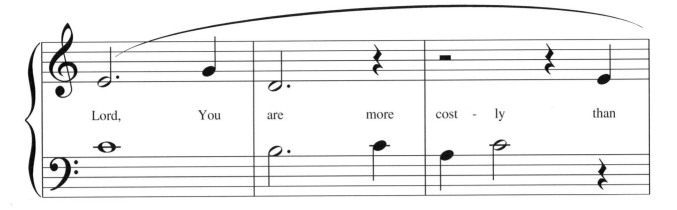

Lord, You are more cost - ly than

gold. *mp* Lord, You are more

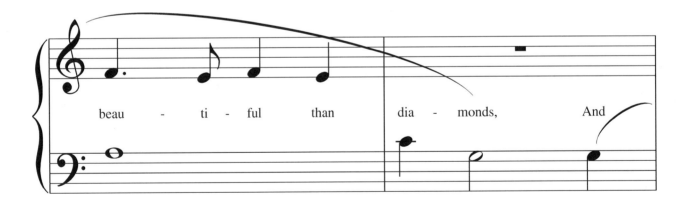

beau - ti - ful than dia - monds, And

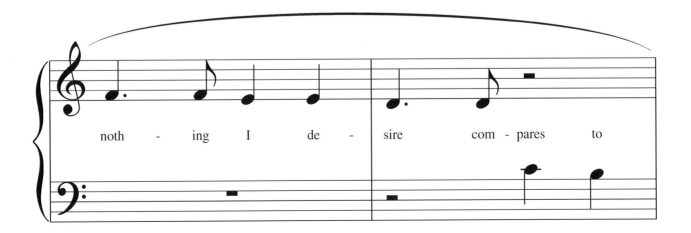

noth - ing I de - sire com - pares to

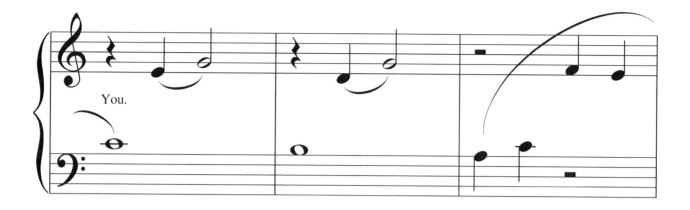

You.

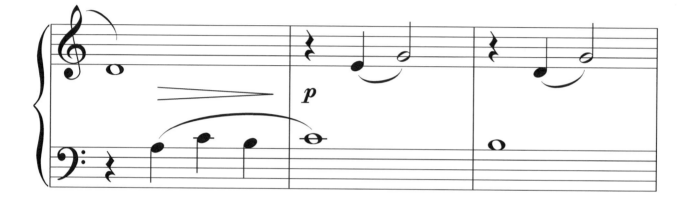

p

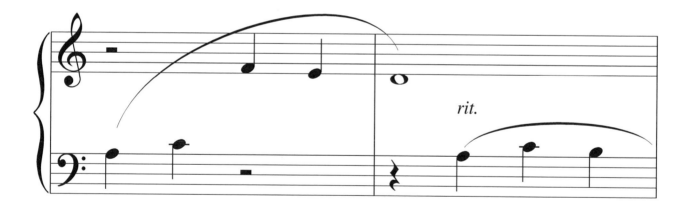

rit.

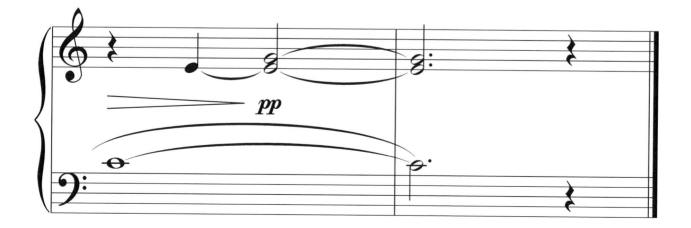

pp

OH HOW HE LOVES YOU AND ME

Words and Music by KURT KAISER
Arranged by Phillip Keveren

Serenely

Oh how He loves you and
Je - sus He to Cal - v'ry did

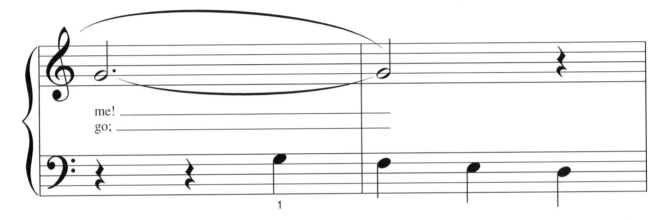

me! _____
go; _____

Oh how He loves you and
His love He for sin - ners to

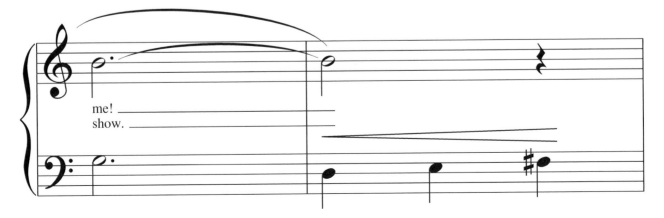

me! _____
show.

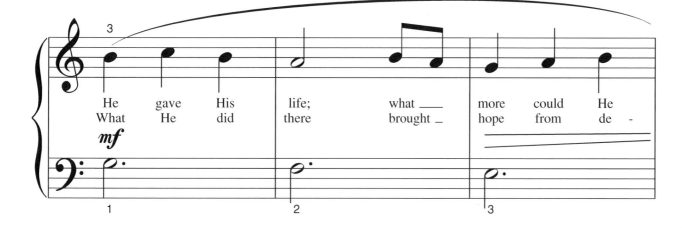

He gave His life; what ___ more could He
What He did there brought _ hope from He de -

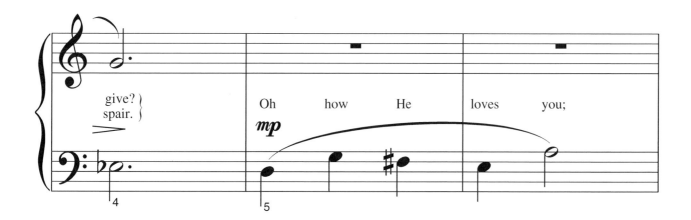

give?
spair.

Oh how He loves you;

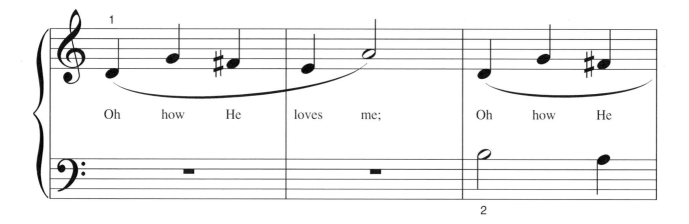

Oh how He loves me; Oh how He

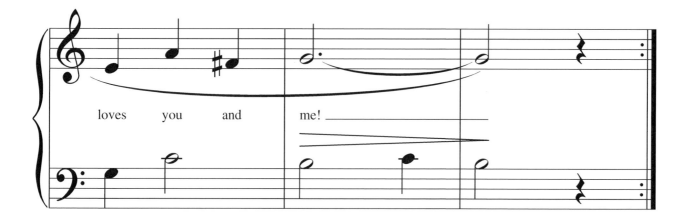

loves you and me! ___

SHOUT TO THE LORD

Words and Music by DARLENE ZSCHECH
Arranged by Phillip Keveren

Majestically

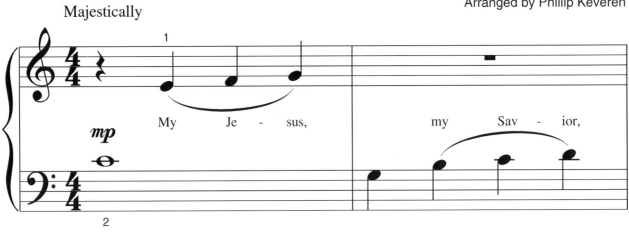

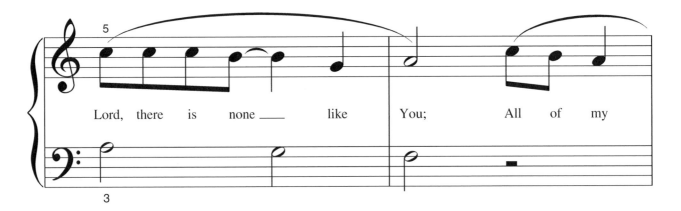

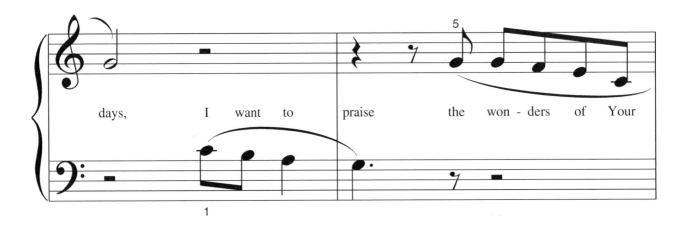

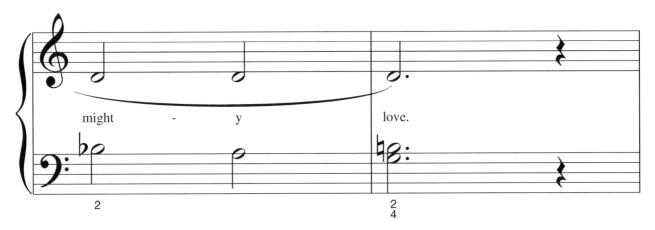

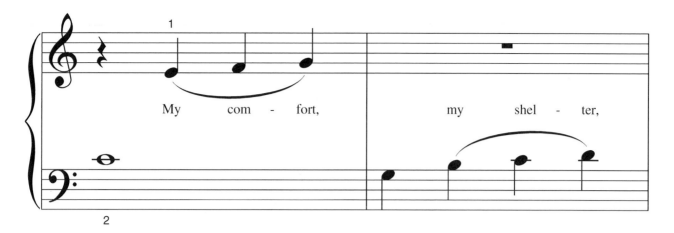

My com - fort, my shel - ter,

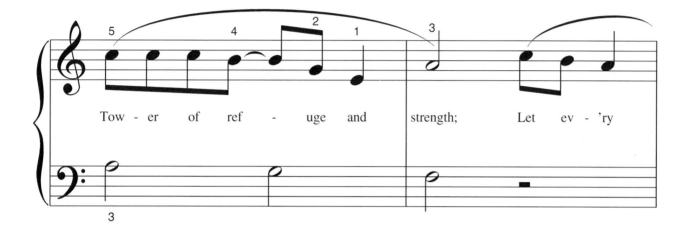

Tow - er of ref - uge and strength; Let ev - 'ry

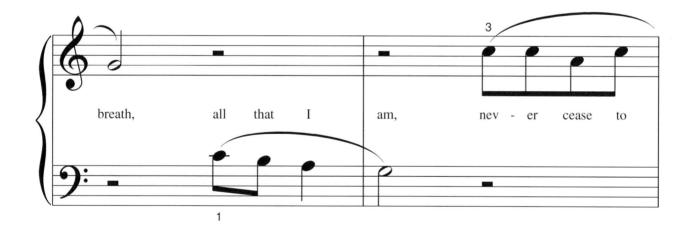

breath, all that I am, nev - er cease to

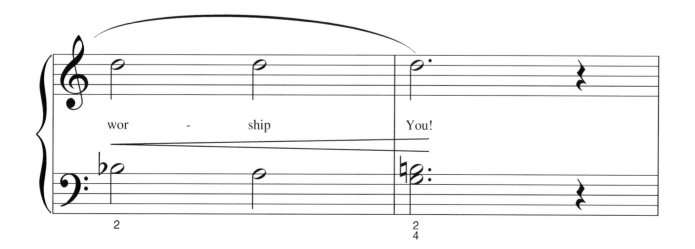

wor - ship You!

44

Shout to the Lord, ___ all the earth, let us sing, ___

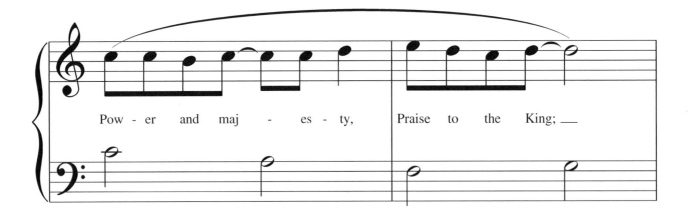

Pow - er and maj - es - ty, Praise to the King; ___

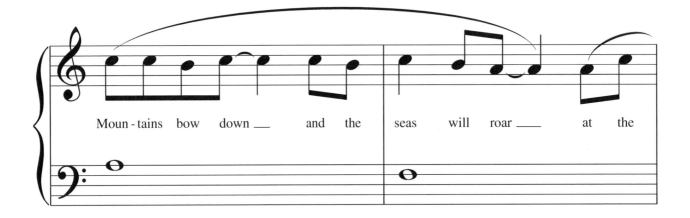

Moun - tains bow down ___ and the seas will roar ___ at the

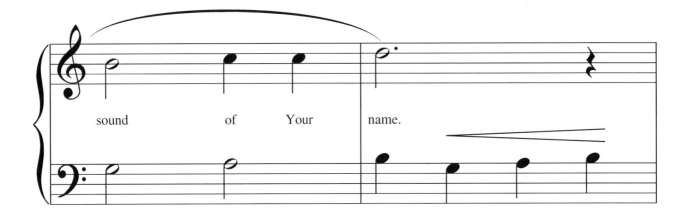

sound of Your name.

I sing for joy ____ at the work of Your hands; ____ For -

ev - er I'll love ____ You, for - ev - er I'll stand! ____

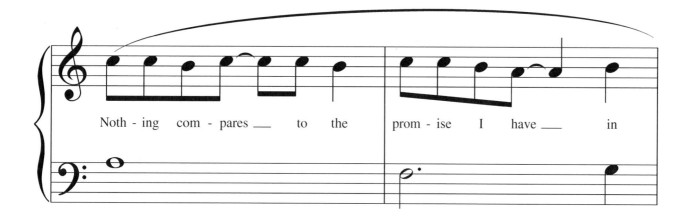

Noth - ing com - pares ____ to the prom - ise I have ____ in

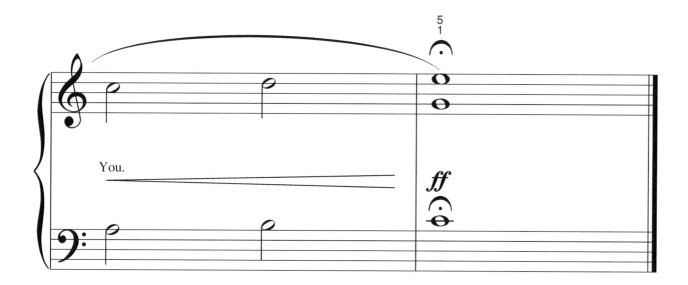

You. ____

ff

THERE IS A REDEEMER

Words and Music by MELODY GREEN
Arranged by Phillip Keveren

Slowly

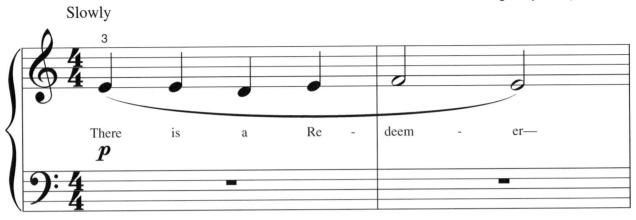

There is a Re- deem- er—

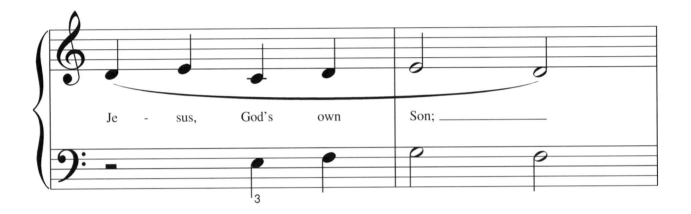

Je- sus, God's own Son; _____

Pre- cious Lamb of God, Mes- si- ah,

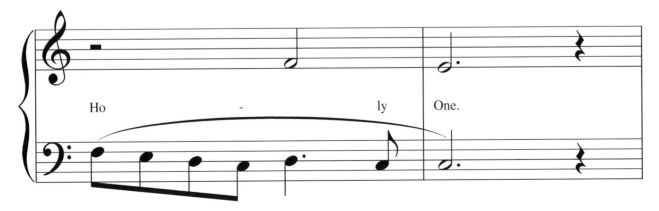

Ho- ly One.

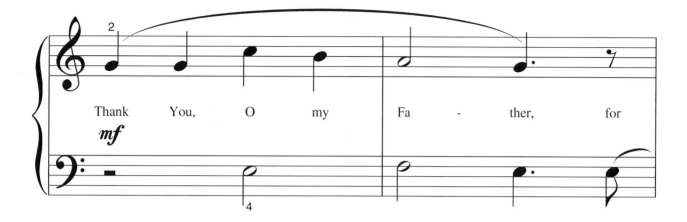

Thank You, O my Fa - ther, for

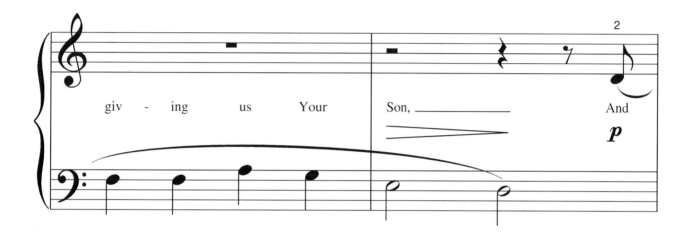

giv - ing us Your Son, _____ And

leav - ing Your Spir - it till the

work ___ on ___ earth is done.

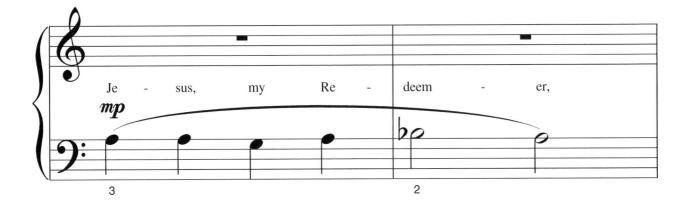

Je - sus, my Re - deem - er,

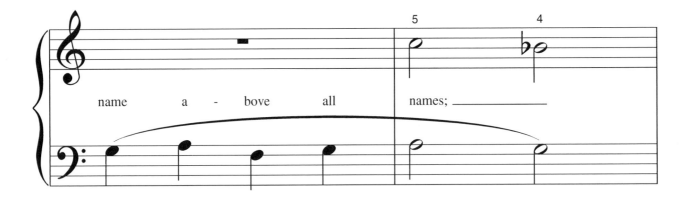

name a - bove all names; ___

Pre - cious Lamb of God, Mes - si - ah,

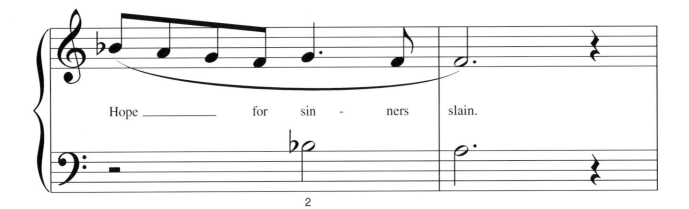

Hope ___ for sin - ners slain.

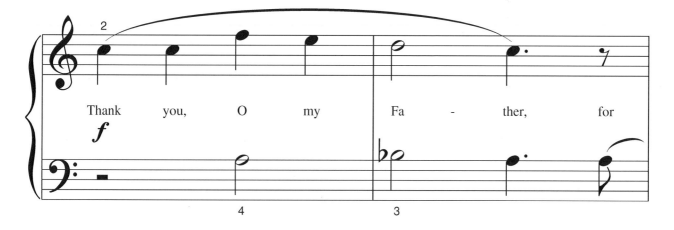

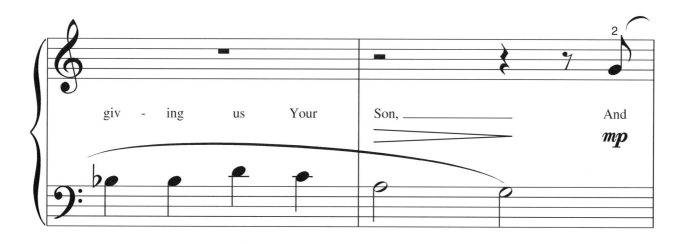

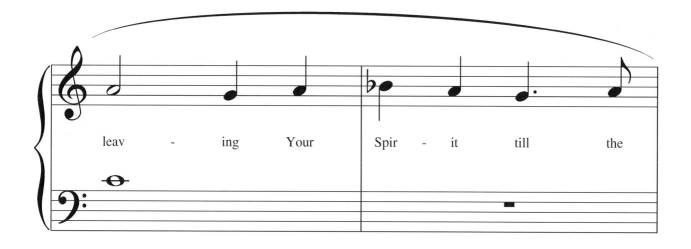

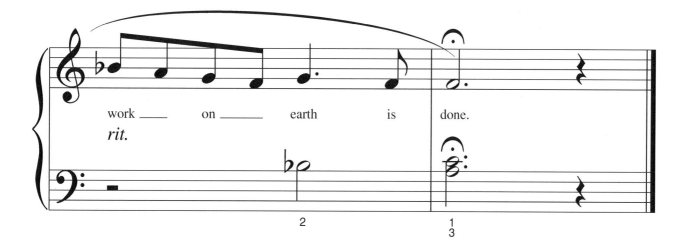

SHOUT TO THE NORTH

Words and Music by MARTIN SMITH
Arranged by Phillip Keveren

Spirited

Men of

faith, rise up and sing
wom - en of the truth,

of the great and glo - rious
stand and sing to bro - ken

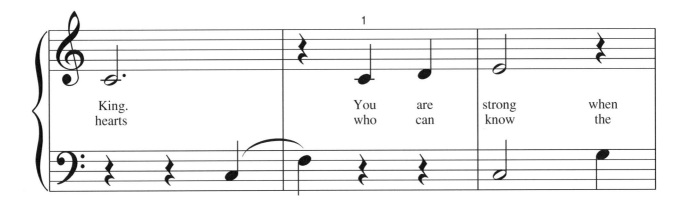

King. You are strong when
hearts who can know the

you feel weak, in your bro - ken -
heal - ing pow'r of our awe - some

ness com - plete.
King of love.

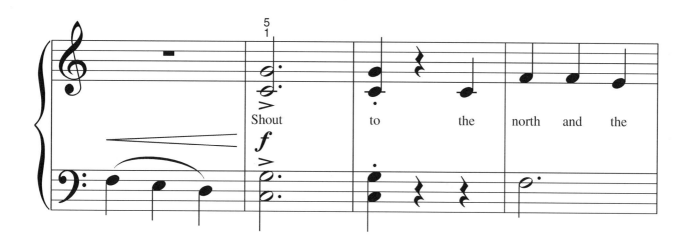

Shout to the north and the

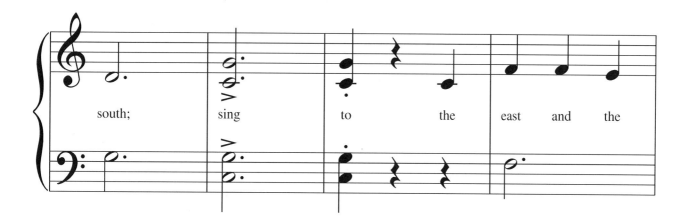

south; sing to the east and the

52

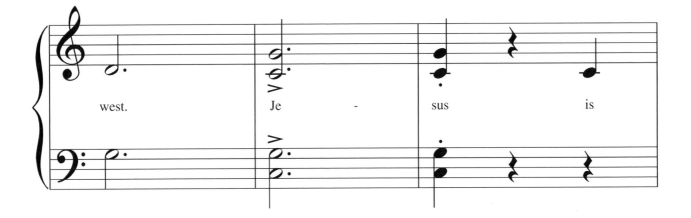

west. Je - sus is

Sav - ior to all, Lord of

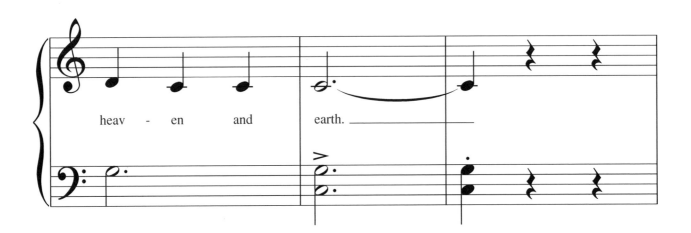

heav - en and earth.

Rise up

WE FALL DOWN

Words and Music by CHRIS TOMLIN
Arranged by Phillip Keveren

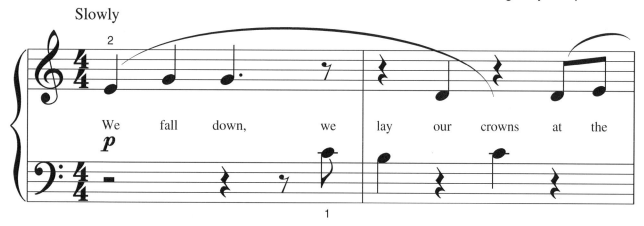

We fall down, we lay our crowns at the

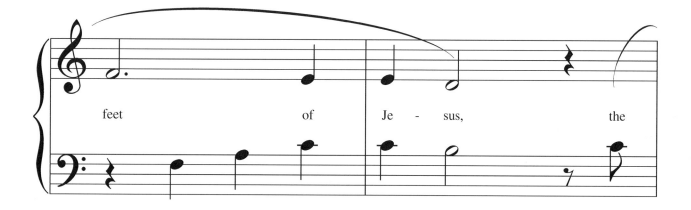

feet of Je - sus, the

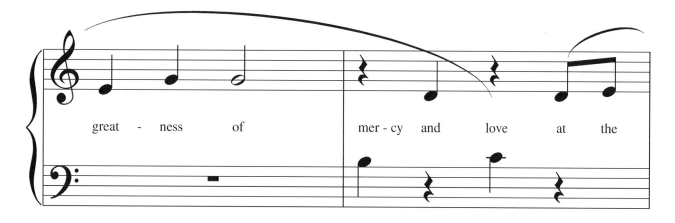

great - ness of mer - cy and love at the

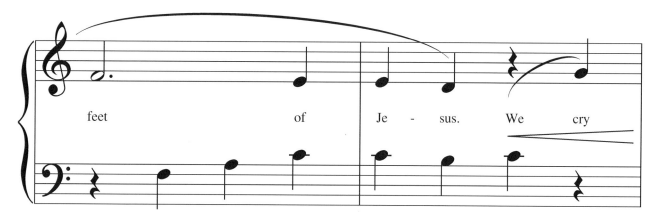

feet of Je - sus. We cry

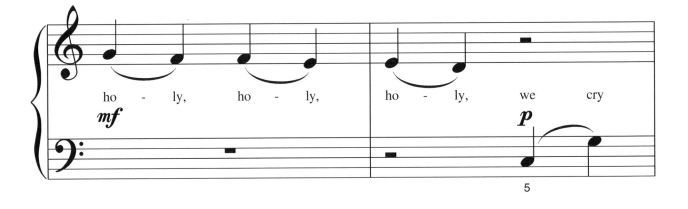

ho - ly, ho - ly, ho - ly, we cry
mf *p*
5

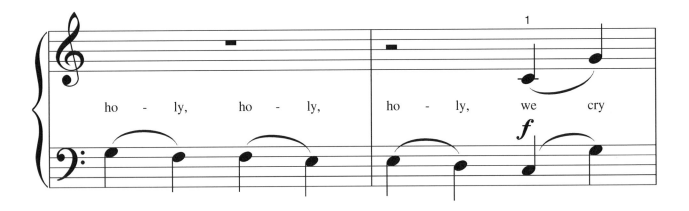

ho - ly, ho - ly, ho - ly, we cry
1
f

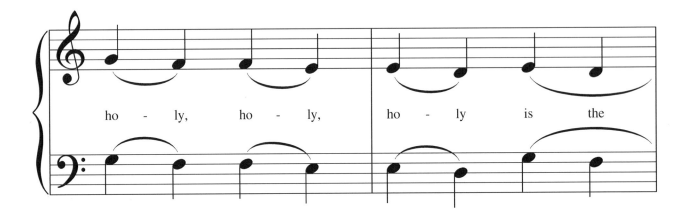

ho - ly, ho - ly, ho - ly is the

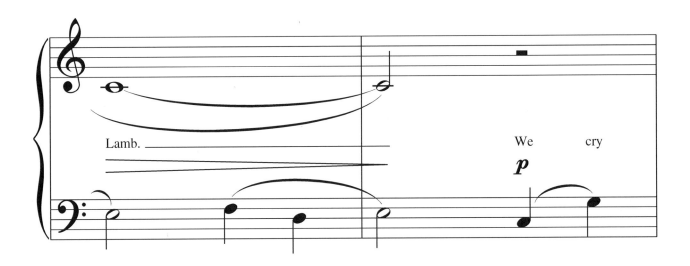

Lamb. We cry
p

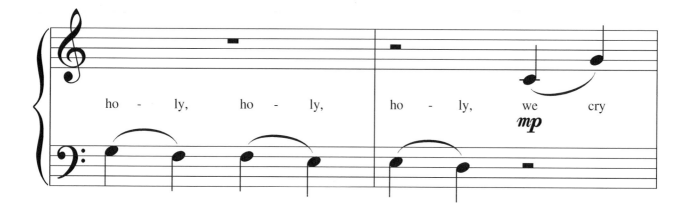

ho - ly, ho - ly, ho - ly, we cry
mp

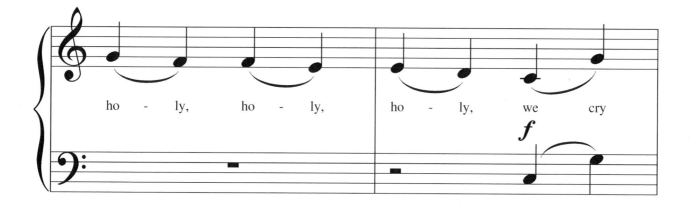

ho - ly, ho - ly, ho - ly, we cry
f

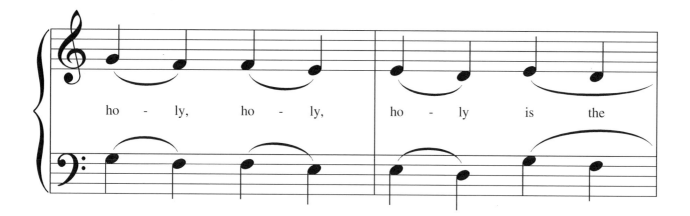

ho - ly, ho - ly, ho - ly is the

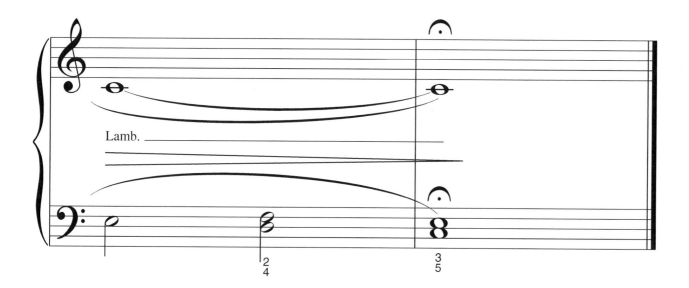

Lamb.

THE PHILLIP KEVEREN SERIES

PIANO SOLO

00156644	**ABBA for Classical Piano**	$15.99
00311024	**Above All**	$12.99
00311348	**Americana**	$12.99
00198473	**Bach Meets Jazz**	$14.99
00313594	**Bacharach and David**	$15.99
00306412	**The Beatles**	$19.99
00312189	**The Beatles for Classical Piano**	$17.99
00275876	**The Beatles – Recital Suites**	$19.99
00312546	**Best Piano Solos**	$15.99
00156601	**Blessings**	$14.99
00198656	**Blues Classics**	$14.99
00284359	**Broadway Songs with a Classical Flair**	$14.99
00310669	**Broadway's Best**	$16.99
00312106	**Canzone Italiana**	$12.99
00280848	**Carpenters**	$17.99
00310629	**A Celtic Christmas**	$14.99
00310549	**The Celtic Collection**	$14.99
00280571	**Celtic Songs with a Classical Flair**	$12.99
00263362	**Charlie Brown Favorites**	$14.99
00312190	**Christmas at the Movies**	$15.99
00294754	**Christmas Carols with a Classical Flair**	$12.99
00311414	**Christmas Medleys**	$14.99
00236669	**Christmas Praise Hymns**	$12.99
00233788	**Christmas Songs for Classical Piano**	$14.99
00311769	**Christmas Worship Medleys**	$14.99
00310607	**Cinema Classics**	$15.99
00301857	**Circles**	$10.99
00311101	**Classic Wedding Songs**	$12.99
00311292	**Classical Folk**	$10.95
00311083	**Classical Jazz**	$14.99
00137779	**Coldplay for Classical Piano**	$16.99
00311103	**Contemporary Wedding Songs**	$12.99
00348788	**Country Songs with a Classical Flair**	$14.99
00249097	**Disney Recital Suites**	$17.99
00311754	**Disney Songs for Classical Piano**	$17.99
00241379	**Disney Songs for Ragtime Piano**	$17.99
00364812	**The Essential Hymn Anthology**	$34.99
00311881	**Favorite Wedding Songs**	$14.99
00315974	**Fiddlin' at the Piano**	$12.99
00311811	**The Film Score Collection**	$15.99
00269408	**Folksongs with a Classical Flair**	$12.99
00144353	**The Gershwin Collection**	$14.99
00233789	**Golden Scores**	$14.99
00144351	**Gospel Greats**	$14.99
00183566	**The Great American Songbook**	$14.99
00312084	**The Great Melodies**	$14.99
00311157	**Great Standards**	$14.99
00171621	**A Grown-Up Christmas List**	$14.99
00311071	**The Hymn Collection**	$14.99
00311349	**Hymn Medleys**	$14.99
00280705	**Hymns in a Celtic Style**	$14.99

00269407	**Hymns with a Classical Flair**	$14.99
00311249	**Hymns with a Touch of Jazz**	$14.99
00310905	**I Could Sing of Your Love Forever**	$16.99
00310762	**Jingle Jazz**	$15.99
00175310	**Billy Joel for Classical Piano**	$16.99
00126449	**Elton John for Classical Piano**	$19.99
00310839	**Let Freedom Ring!**	$12.99
00238988	**Andrew Lloyd Webber Piano Songbook**	$14.99
00313227	**Andrew Lloyd Webber Solos**	$17.99
00313523	**Mancini Magic**	$16.99
00312113	**More Disney Songs for Classical Piano**	$16.99
00311295	**Motown Hits**	$14.99
00300640	**Piano Calm**	$12.99
00339131	**Piano Calm: Christmas**	$14.99
00346009	**Piano Calm: Prayer**	$14.99
00306870	**Piazzolla Tangos**	$17.99
00386709	**Praise and Worship for Classical Piano**	$14.99
00156645	**Queen for Classical Piano**	$17.99
00310755	**Richard Rodgers Classics**	$17.99
00289545	**Scottish Songs**	$12.99
00119403	**The Sound of Music**	$16.99
00311978	**The Spirituals Collection**	$12.99
00366023	**So Far...**	$14.99
00210445	**Star Wars**	$16.99
00224738	**Symphonic Hymns for Piano**	$14.99
00366022	**Three-Minute Encores**	$16.99
00279673	**Tin Pan Alley**	$12.99
00312112	**Treasured Hymns for Classical Piano**	$15.99
00144926	**The Twelve Keys of Christmas**	$14.99
00278486	**The Who for Classical Piano**	$16.99
00294036	**Worship with a Touch of Jazz**	$14.99
00311911	**Yuletide Jazz**	$19.99

EASY PIANO

00210401	**Adele for Easy Classical Piano**	$17.99
00310610	**African-American Spirituals**	$12.99
00218244	**The Beatles for Easy Classical Piano**	$14.99
00218387	**Catchy Songs for Piano**	$12.99
00310973	**Celtic Dreams**	$12.99
00233686	**Christmas Carols for Easy Classical Piano**	$14.99
00311126	**Christmas Pops**	$16.99
00368199	**Christmas Reflections**	$14.99
00311548	**Classic Pop/Rock Hits**	$14.99
00310769	**A Classical Christmas**	$14.99
00310975	**Classical Movie Themes**	$12.99
00144352	**Disney Songs for Easy Classical Piano**	$14.99
00311093	**Early Rock 'n' Roll**	$14.99
00311997	**Easy Worship Medleys**	$14.99
00289547	**Duke Ellington**	$14.99
00160297	**Folksongs for Easy Classical Piano**	$12.99

00110374	**George Gershwin Classics**	$14.99
00310805	**Gospel Treasures**	$14.99
00306821	**Vince Guaraldi Collection**	$19.99
00160294	**Hymns for Easy Classical Piano**	$14.99
00310798	**Immortal Hymns**	$12.99
00311294	**Jazz Standards**	$12.99
00355474	**Living Hope**	$14.99
00310744	**Love Songs**	$14.99
00233740	**The Most Beautiful Songs for Easy Classical Piano**	$12.99
00220036	**Pop Ballads**	$14.99
00311406	**Pop Gems of the 1950s**	$12.95
00233739	**Pop Standards for Easy Classical Piano**	$12.99
00102887	**A Ragtime Christmas**	$12.99
00311293	**Ragtime Classics**	$14.99
00312028	**Santa Swings**	$14.99
00233688	**Songs from Childhood for Easy Classical Piano**	$12.99
00103258	**Songs of Inspiration**	$14.99
00310840	**Sweet Land of Liberty**	$12.99
00126450	**10,000 Reasons**	$16.99
00310712	**Timeless Praise**	$14.99
00311086	**TV Themes**	$14.99
00310717	**21 Great Classics**	$14.99
00160076	**Waltzes & Polkas for Easy Classical Piano**	$12.99
00145342	**Weekly Worship**	$17.99

BIG-NOTE PIANO

00310838	**Children's Favorite Movie Songs**	$14.99
00346000	**Christmas Movie Magic**	$12.99
00277368	**Classical Favorites**	$12.99
00277370	**Disney Favorites**	$14.99
00310888	**Joy to the World**	$12.99
00310908	**The Nutcracker**	$12.99
00277371	**Star Wars**	$16.99

BEGINNING PIANO SOLOS

00311202	**Awesome God**	$14.99
00310837	**Christian Children's Favorites**	$14.99
00311117	**Christmas Traditions**	$10.99
00311250	**Easy Hymns**	$12.99
00102710	**Everlasting God**	$10.99
00311403	**Jazzy Tunes**	$10.95
00310822	**Kids' Favorites**	$12.99
00367778	**A Magical Christmas**	$14.99
00338175	**Silly Songs for Kids**	$9.99

PIANO DUET

00126452	**The Christmas Variations**	$14.99
00362562	**Classic Piano Duets**	$14.99
00311350	**Classical Theme Duets**	$12.99
00295099	**Gospel Duets**	$12.99
00311544	**Hymn Duets**	$14.99
00311203	**Praise & Worship Duets**	$14.99
00294755	**Sacred Christmas Duets**	$14.99
00119405	**Star Wars**	$16.99
00253545	**Worship Songs for Two**	$12.99

Prices, contents, and availability subject to change without notice.